The No-Bullying Program

Preventing Bully/Victim Violence at School

Teacher's Manual For Grades 4 & 5

James Bitney—Curriculum Writer

Beverly B. Title, Ph.D.—Program Developer

JOHNSON INSTITUTE®

Minneapolis

Acknowledgment

The contents of this book are based on the No-Bullying Curriculum model originally developed for the St. Vrain Valley School District, Longmont, Colorado, by Beverly B. Title, with assistance from Lisa Anderson-Goebel, Vivian Bray, K.G. Campanella-Green, Ted Goodwin, Karen Greene, Elizabeth Martinson, Mike O'Connell, and Peggy Stortz.

The Bullying Behavior Chart was developed by Beverly B. Title, Ph.D.; Severance Kelly, M.D.; Louis Krupnik, Ph.D.; Joseph Matthews, M.S.W.; Kendra Bartley, M.A.

Curriculum consultation was provided by Peggy O'Connell.

The No-Bullying Program: Preventing Bully/Victim Violence at School

Teacher's Manual for Grades 4 & 5

James Bitney, Curriculum Writer
Beverly B. Title, Ph.D., Program Developer

Johnson Institute
7205 Ohms Lane
Minneapolis, Minnesota 55439-2159
612-831-1630 or 800-231-5165

ISBN 1-56246-121-4

Logo design: Diana Garcia
Cover and text design: Crombie Design
Artwork by Sally Brewer Lawrence
Printed in the United States of America
96 97 98 99 / 5 4 3 2 1

Contents

INTRODUCTION
School Zones—Danger Zones

In 1991, 25,000 people were murdered in the United States. During that same year, there were over 67 million handguns in the United States. Sadly, many of the most heavily armed are young people. One official described the arming of America's teenagers as a real "arms race" in which "no one wants to be left behind." Many schools list weapons on campus as one of their top concerns. An eighth grader in a Connecticut junior high school was suspended for refusing to remove his hat. The next day, he came to school with an assault rifle, killed the janitor and wounded the principal and the school secretary.

> A thirteen year old in Florida threatened to torture and kill his social studies teacher after receiving a poor grade on a test. When the boy was arrested, he had two pistols, a box of bullets, and a switchblade.

> After losing a very close foot race, an eighth-grade girl shot the winner, a classmate, in the leg, claiming, "She cheated."

Violence threatens the fiber of our education system both for teachers and for students. In some schools, gun fights have replaced fist fights and "bullet drills" have replaced fire drills. Guns aren't the only weapons at school. Students have been caught with knives, razors, even bombs. Students say they carry weapons for protection. In 1991, over 3 million young people became the victims of violent crime at school.

Teachers do not fare much better than students. A report from the National Education Association indicates that every month of the school year 12% of teachers will have something stolen, 6,000 will have something taken from them forcefully, 120,000 will be threatened, 5,200 will be attacked, and 19% of those attacked will require medical attention.

Violence: A Definition

These startling statistics point out that too many students and teachers are unsafe in their own schools. Too many use violence, witness violence, or are victims of violence. Unfortunately, violence means different things to different people. That is why the Johnson Institute has sought to define violence as:

Any word, look, sign, or act that inflicts or threatens to inflict physical or emotional injury or discomfort upon another person's body, feelings, or possessions.

Violence: A Delineation

Basically, there are two types of violence: peer violence and bully/victim violence.

- Peer violence is defined as acts of violence stemming from disagreements, misunderstandings, or conflicting desires among students who are equally matched in strength and power.

- Bully/victim violence involves an imbalance of power and strength between students; bully/victim violence occurs whenever a student intentionally, repeatedly, and over time inflicts or threatens to inflict physical or emotional injury or discomfort on another's body, feelings, or possessions.

Both kinds must be dealt with to make our schools safe.

Dealing with Bully/Victim Violence: The No-Bullying Program

Schools can successfully deal with the problem of peer violence by helping students grow in social skills: communication, feeling processing, problem solving, conflict management, and conflict mediation. Unfortunately, schools have not been so successful in dealing with bully/victim violence.

The No-Bullying Program has been designed to provide a research-based, educational model to deal with bully/victim violence in the school. Research has clearly shown that bullies do not respond to social skill work. Bullies do not care that what they are doing is creating problems for others. In fact, they generally enjoy the results of their bullying behavior. *The No-Bullying Program* offers schools a plan for dealing with bullies and bully/victim violence.

Approximately 15% of any school population are bullies or victims of bullies, which means that 85% of the school population are relatively uninvolved in bullying behaviors. To end bullying, the *No-Bullying Program* engages the help of that 85% by:

- Clearly defining what is and what is not bullying

- Creating empathy for the victims of bullying

- Teaching students when and how to report bullying

- Establishing clear consequences for bullying that are strictly enforced by everyone in the school

To assure the help of that 85%, the *No-Bullying Program* also insists that *all adults* in the school take more proactive roles in dealing with bullies and their victims. Research has shown that adult intervention is crucial to ending bully/victim violence. Once students realize that reporting bullying to an adult will result in immediate intervention and action (consequences), they feel secure in becoming proactive in ending bullying themselves.

Prior to meeting with the students, you have met with *all* school staff and support staff to:

- overview the *No-Bullying Program* in its entirety

- review research and correct misinformation about bullying: its perpetrators and its victims

- learn how to stop enabling bullying behavior

- agree on a school-wide policy of no-entitlement and no-tolerance with regard to bullying behaviors

- learn intervention strategies with regard to bullying behaviors

- create support networks with community leaders and service providers, professionals in the areas of violence and domestic abuse, law enforcement officials, student leaders, and parent advisory group leaders or members

- establish a procedure enabling the students to feel safe when reporting bullying

- set, and commit to the consistent enforcement of, school-wide consequences for bullying behaviors

Now, as a teacher, your role in the project is to lead the students through an exciting educational process designed to empower them to end bullying in their school and to make it "Safe Zone" for learning.

How to Use This Manual

This *Teacher's Manual* offers you material and detailed guidance to lead fourth and fifth graders through six 30- to 40-minute sessions of interactive learning. You may lengthen or shorten the session time, depending on the deletion or addition of an activity and your particular teaching style.

Aims of the Program

To teach strategically formulated awarenesses and skills that are designed to help the students:

- understand the *No-Bullying Program*

- define bullying, disclose personal experiences with bully/victim problems, and heighten their awareness of these problems

- define and enumerate bullying behaviors

- develop empathy for the victims of bullying

- recognize the distinction between tattling and telling in order to get help in a bullying situation

- learn the school-wide consequences for engaging in bullying behaviors

Learning Strategies

The *No-Bullying Program* incorporates a variety of strategies to help you facilitate learning. These strategies include:

- Kinesthetic learning tactics

- Brainstorming

- Drama and role playing

- Group discussion

- Teaching Masters

Kinesthetic Learning Tactics

An ancient Oriental proverb states: "Tell me, I'll forget. Show me, I may remember. But involve me, and I'll understand." Put simply, kinesthetic learning techniques *involve* the students. Using these techniques allows you to appeal to more than one sense of the learner. They even allow you to get learners moving, so that body muscles may respond to the learning stimuli.

When the students hear you say something and, at the same time, see some information you've printed on the board or newsprint, they retain more of that you're saying. As you teach, then, frequently write out words and terms as you say them. Likewise, capture attention by using sight as well as hearing. If you write a word or term, circle, star, box, underline, or check it if you refer to it a second or third time. Draw lines and arrows to connect words—to draw connections between terms. Consider using different colored chalk or markers to show relationships or connections between words and terms. This does more than add color; it makes relationships stand out.

Avail yourself of every opportunity to get the students on their feet, raise their hands, turn in their seats. Encourage them to use all their senses as they learn.

Brainstorming

Brainstorming allows everyone to speak quickly and briefly and puts the burden of knowledge on no one person. Brainstorming is proof of the adage that "All of us are smarter than any one of us." Brainstorming is an activity that's easy to do and with which almost all students are comfortable, since every brainstorming response or idea is an acceptable one.

When the students brainstorm, list their responses (or words that describe them) on the board or newsprint, but don't add your comments; for example: "Good!" "Just what I was thinking." "I don't see how that fits, but I'll write it down anyway." "Do you really mean that?" Your comments, either positive or negative, can prevent some students from saying anything or can embarrass others. Be aware that as the students brainstorm, a type of synergism takes place. Initial responses elicit new responses that pull together many ideas into one. This synergism tends to energize the students and make them eager to join in.

When brainstorming, be wary of searching for "the right response" and then stopping the brainstorming once somebody gives it. Instead, set a time limit for brainstorming and get all the responses you can during that time. Or simply end the brainstorming when the students stop coming up with ideas.

Finally, brainstorming helps students realize that they already know a great deal, that the answers to questions they may have already lie within them. Thus brainstorming helps the students value themselves and appreciate that you value them.

Drama and Role Playing

In drama (skits) and role playing, students assume various characters and create roles. During role play, they may explore situations, identify problems, resolve conflicts, and create solutions. In other words, they deal with real-life matters in a safe situation. They can experience a whole range of emotions as they identify with characters and roles and work toward creative solutions. These activities can provide insights for the students that simple discussion cannot.

At the conclusion of a drama (skit) or role play, always offer those who took part the opportunity to express and process their feelings. Likewise offer the observers the chance to share their observations and perceptions.

Group Discussion

In group discussion a synergy that is more than just the sum of the number of students in the group can result from their talking together and sharing ideas. The sum becomes more than the addition of its parts.

Teaching Masters

This level of the *No-Bullying Program* provides you with 12 Teaching Masters (see pages 44–55), which you can reproduce as handouts for the students. The students use them as worksheets to explore the key concepts of a particular session.

Understanding the Nine- to Eleven-year-old Child

For the most part, the following characteristics—all of which are *normal*—are exhibited by the nine- to eleven-year-old child. He or she:

- is beginning to identify strongly with his or her peer group and its interests

- continues to seek and need parental/adult encouragement and approval

- wants to live by rules and wants others to do likewise (fairness/reciprocity is paramount)

- generally can differentiate between right and wrong, especially through formularies such as rules and regulations

- seeks to tell the truth, but sometimes avoids speaking rather than lying

- has one or two close friends of the same sex

- does not like to be identified with the opposite sex

- is beginning to be interested in sexuality

- is able to observe people and situations and form conclusions about them

- continues to think concretely, but is beginning to think abstractly in some areas (e.g., physical science, math)

- can play games and sports with more complex rules

- seeks increasing independence from family, yet relies on it as a security base

- talks back to adults, especially family members

- wants to be "in on" things, especially family plans, school plans, etc.

- likes to joke, act silly, play with double meanings in language

- exhibits temper, but generally is able to control it

- is sensitive toward criticism, but can see that criticism can be useful

- is both proud of and embarrassed by parental comments made in the presence of others; sometimes has trouble sorting out these ambivalent feelings

- is becoming more and more aware of the perspective or feelings of others

- still exhibits shyness around unfamiliar people

- needs privacy at times

Session Components

- **Aim** states the overall goal of the session.

- **Objectives** lists the learning outcomes of the session.

- **Materials** catalogues all the teaching devices necessary to present the session.

- **Preparing for the Session** contains directions for all the pre-session arrangements necessary to present the session.

- **Background for the Teacher** includes pertinent information:

  — to help you set the educational content in context

  — to provide you with added information for personal growth

  — to give you new data necessary to present the session with the greatest success.

- **Session Plan** includes the specific steps or directions for presenting the session. Each **Session Plan** is composed of three parts: *Beginning the Session, Leading the Session,* and *Concluding the Session.*

  — *Beginning the Session* serves to welcome and gather the students, unite them as a group, review previous learning, and get them ready to work and share together.

  — *Leading the Session* includes learning activities, discussions, exercises, drama or role play, as well as other educational processes, presented in a clear, step-by-step design that enables you to guide the students through the session.

  — *Concluding the Session,* which remains relatively the same for every session, includes activities that serve to affirm the students in what they learned during the session and to help them commit themselves to No-Bullying both as individuals and as a school community.

Finally, some of the plans include one or more Optional Activities, which you may choose to use to replace an activity in the plan, to enhance the plan, or to extend the session.

This session plan format strives to give the students a total experience that is structured but hospitable, instructive but creative, and challenging but supportive. Because the format remains constant for each session, it also meets the needs of at-risk students for structure, stability, consistency, and enjoyment. You may use the plans with confidence.

Session 1

Aim

To introduce the *No-Bullying Program* to the students

Objectives

By the end of the session, the students will

- recognize and understand the No-Bullying logo

- begin to identify bullying and its effects

- appreciate that their school is committed to ending bullying

Materials

- copy of the No-Bullying logo poster (Teaching Master 1)

- copies of the No-Bullying logos (Teaching Master 2)

- copies of "Bully Not Wanted" (Teaching Master 3)

- "The No-Bullying Pledge" poster

- newsprint and marker

- newspaper want ad sheets

- pens or pencils

- paste or glue sticks

- blank index cards

- optional: construction paper for bumper stickers

Preparing for the Session

Carefully read over the session plan in advance. Make a copy of the No-Bullying logo poster (Teaching Master 1) to be used throughout the sessions. Make copies of the No-Bullying Logos (Teaching Master 2), enough so that each student can have his or her own logo—there are four to a page. Cut out the individual logos prior to the session. Have a "want ad" page of your local newspaper for each student. Make copies of "Bully Not Wanted" (Teaching Master 3), one for each student. Using a large sheet of newsprint and markers, make a poster of "The No-Bullying Pledge" on page 13. Have a pen or pencil, paste or a glue stick, and a blank index card for each child.

Finally, if you choose to use the Optional Activity, arrange to have the appropriate materials on hand, and make any necessary adjustments to the Session Plan.

Background for the Teacher

It is important for you, as a teacher, to understand that bullying is not always obvious. It most often takes place in concealed areas. At school, bullying occurs where you're not present or where you can't see: in bathrooms, in hallways, on playground areas that are difficult to supervise, in empty classrooms, etc. Simply because you do not witness bullying behaviors does not mean they aren't taking place.

Session Plan

Beginning the Session

Gather the students in a circle. Join the circle yourself. Introduce yourself and offer your own words of welcome. Then, beginning with the student on your right, go around the circle, having each student introduce himself or herself, mention what he or she most likes and least likes about school, and then tell one thing that makes him or her feel safe at school.

Leading the Session

1. Display the copy of the No-Bullying logo poster. Ask the students what they think it may mean. Accept all replies and list them on newsprint.

2. Draw on the students' ideas to lead a discussion about the logo with the group. Encourage the students to share:

   • what types of things they think bullying children do

- what happens to children who bully others

- what happens to children who are being bullied

- how bullying affects their school.

Again, as you discuss, list children's ideas on newsprint.

3. After the discussion, tell the students that they will be talking more about bullying behavior—about students taking unfair advantage of others—for the next few weeks. Point out that your school is committed to stopping all bullying and getting hurt by bullying in your school. Then say:

> "In our class time together, we will learn how to help each other, and we'll learn the best ways to get help to end bullying. However, whenever we talk about bullying *in this class*, we will never call anyone by name who is bullying or being bullied."

4. Pass out the newspaper want ads you gathered prior to the session. If necessary, take a moment to explain the purpose of want ads to the students. Invite different students to read aloud one of the want ads on their newspaper sheets. Afterward, use the board or newsprint to point out how a want ad generally does all of the following:

- names a job or position to be filled

- lists the experience necessary to do the job

- lists job responsibilities or duties (what a person in the job has to do)

- gives the salary and benefits for the job (what the job pays)

- tells where to apply for the job

Go on to tell the students that they are going to write some want ads, but that they will be making *reverse want ads*.

5. Distribute pens or pencils, cut-outs of the No-Bullying logos (from Teaching Master 2), paste or glue sticks, and copies of "Bully Not Wanted" (Teaching Master 3). Explain to the students that they are to make a not-wanted ad for bullies and bullying in their school.

Drawing on the students' responses to the discussion in Step 1, lead them through the not-wanted ad writing activity:

- For "Experience Necessary," have the students list what they thought bullying children do (for example, hitting, name-calling, threatening, etc.).

- For "Job Duties," have the students list how bullying affects children who are being bullied and their whole school (for example, makes little kids afraid).

- For "Pay/Benefits," have the students list what they feel happens to children who bully others (for example, no friends or lots of detention).

- For the final line, "Do **Not** Apply At," direct the students to fill in the name of their school.

To complete the activity, have the students paste or glue the cut-out No-Bullying logo in the space indicated on the page, then write their names on the back. Encourage students to share their not-wanted ads with the group. Then collect them along with the paste or glue sticks. Tell the students that you will post their "Bully Not Wanted" ads throughout the school.

Note: After the session, and before posting the students' not-wanted ads, read through them. What the students wrote will help to give you a fairly accurate picture of how they presently view bullying. You can draw on and build on these perceptions as you present information in the sessions to come.

6. Pass out blank index cards. Display the poster of the No-Bullying pledge you made prior to the session so all can see it. Read the pledge aloud:

THE NO-BULLYING PLEDGE

Here in our school,

No bullying for us.

No hurting for us.

No unfairness for us.

No bullying for us,

No, not in our school.

Have the students copy the pledge on the index cards. Encourage them to carry the card with them and to commit the pledge to memory. Explain that they will be using this pledge to conclude their meeting times together.

Collect pens or pencils.

Concluding the Session

Have the students form a circle around you. Set the copy of the No-Bullying logo poster on the floor in the center of the circle. Join the circle yourself, and invite the students to join hands. Explain that you will be sending a "pledge" of support around the circle, a pledge that everyone in the circle can share. Tell the students that you will *gently* squeeze the hand of the person on your right. Then he or she will *gently* squeeze the hand of the person on his or her right, and so on, until the "pledge" of support goes all the way around the circle.

Once the "pledge" has returned to you, invite the students to show that they pledge to support no bullying in their school by taking a step forward—thus tightening the circle—and by reciting the No-Bullying pledge:

THE NO-BULLYING PLEDGE

Here in our school,

No bullying for us.

No hurting for us.

No unfairness for us.

No bullying for us,

No, not in our school.

Remind the students of the time of their next session, when they will begin to identify bullying behavior and take part in an important survey.

Optional Activity

In lieu of, or in addition to, the "Bully Not Wanted" ads in Step 5, have the students use a copy of the No-Bullying logos (from Teaching Master 2) and construction paper to make bumper stickers (with words or drawings) about bullying. The bumper stickers should warn against or reject bullying, for example, "Have a No-Bullying Day." Display the bumper stickers in the meeting room and throughout the school.

Session 2

Aim

To help the students define bullying, disclose experiences with bully/victim problems, and heighten their awareness of these problems.

Objectives

By the end of the session, the students will

- discover a definition of bullying

- share experience of—and become more aware of—bullying and its effects

- better appreciate how their school is committed to ending bullying

Materials

- copy of the No-Bullying logo poster from Session 1

- chalkboard and chalk or newsprint and marker

- newsprint sheet from Session 1

- posterboard

- copies of the survey, "What's Happening?" (Teaching Master 4)

- pencils

Preparing for the Session

Carefully read through the session plan in advance. With a marker or art letters, on a piece of posterboard, make a poster that reads:

> **BULLYING HAPPENS...**
>
> when someone with *greater* power
>
> *unfairly* hurts someone
>
> with *lesser* power
>
> *over and over again.*

Note: You will need this poster for the remainder of the sessions. Make copies of the survey "What's Happening?" (Teaching Master 4) so that each student has his or her own copy. Make sure that the No-Bullying logo poster is prominently displayed.

Background for the Teacher

Besides using the survey, "What's Happening?" during this session, feel free to re-use it at any time you feel the need to do a perception check on bullying. Whenever you administer the survey, be sure to share results with other school staff. That way, your school will have a broader perspective on the problem.

Session Plan

Beginning the Session

Gather the students in a circle. Draw attention to the copy of the No-Bullying logo poster. Invite volunteers to recall what the logo means. Remind the students that whenever they talk about bullying *in class* they should not call anyone by name who may be bullying or being bullied.

Leading the Session

1. Display the newsprint sheet of the students' ideas, which you saved from Session 1. Briefly go through the material on the sheet, reminding the students of what they thought were:

   • the types of things bullying children do

   • what happens to children who bully others

- what happens to children who are being bullied

- how bullying affects their school.

    Note: Once again, save the sheet for use again in Session 3.

2. Display the "Bullying Happens" poster you prepared prior to the session and read it aloud to the group.

BULLYING HAPPENS...

when someone with *greater* **power**

unfairly **hurts someone**

with *lesser* **power**

over and over again.

Then divide the board or newsprint into three columns, labeling them as follows:

<u>**Physical Strength**</u>   <u>**Verbal Ability**</u>   <u>**Social Skills**</u>

Explain these concepts to the students, using examples of each one. Tell the group that if someone has greater "power" than someone else in any of these three areas and uses that "power" to hurt over and over, that is bullying.

3. Draw attention once again to the newsprint sheet of ideas, which you saved from Session 1 and used in Step 1 above. Drawing on the behaviors the students already described, have them determine what sort of "power" is being used and then list it under the appropriate heading on the board or newsprint. For example:

Physical Strength	Verbal Ability	Social Skills
size	threats	humiliating
hitting	insults	excluding
pushing	name calling	hurting
stealing	teasing	feelings
defacing/destroying property	making fun of another	playing mean tricks

Make sure the students understand that for negative actions to be labeled "bullying," there must be an *imbalance* of power and a *pattern* or *repetition* of conduct. Stress that bullying happens whenever someone *unfairly* uses power to hurt someone else over and over again.

4. Tell the students that now that they have a definition of bullying, they will be completing an important survey about bullying. Make sure they understand that the survey is not a test and that it is anonymous. Explain that the survey simply asks them to respond to statements about their life at school. Point out that there are no right or wrong answers and that some of the items may have more than one answer. Tell the students that as they respond to each statement, they should mark as many answers as apply to them.

5. Distribute pencils and copies of the survey, "What's Happening?" (Teaching Master 4) and direct the students to complete it.

6. When everyone is finished, help the students better "own" the survey by drawing attention to statement #4 (*I think that most of the bullying that happens at our school happens…*). Then ask the students to raise their hands if they checked the first possible response (*in classrooms*). Have one of the students record the number of responses on the board or newsprint. Go on to do the same for the five remaining possible responses. Finally, have the students count up the responses and determine what they, as a group, believe to be the place(s) in their school where most bullying happens.

7. Go on to repeat the above procedure for statement #9 (*To help me feel safe at school, I think adults should…*). Ask a different student to act as recorder.

Afterward, assure the students that you will convey their concerns about where bullying takes place in their school, what they'd like adults to do about it, as well as all other pertinent information from their surveys to other adults in the school, including the principal.

Collect the pencils and surveys.

Note: Be sure to review all the surveys prior to the next session.

Concluding the Session

Have the students form a circle around you. Set the copy of the No-Bullying logo poster on the floor in the center of the circle. Remind the students of the definition of bullying:

> **BULLYING HAPPENS...**
>
> **when someone with *greater* power**
>
> *unfairly* **hurts someone**
>
> **with *lesser* power**
>
> *over and over again.*

Join the circle yourself and have the students join hands. As in the first session, explain that you will be sending a "pledge" of support around the circle, a pledge that everyone in the circle can share. Tell the students that you will *gently* squeeze the hand of the person on your right. Then he or she will *gently* squeeze the hand of the person on his or her right, and so on, until the "pledge" of support goes all the way around the circle.

Once the "pledge" has returned to you, invite the students to show that they pledge to support no bullying in their school by taking a step forward—thus tightening the circle—and by reciting the No-Bullying pledge:

THE NO-BULLYING PLEDGE

Here in our school,

No bullying for us.

No hurting for us.

No unfairness for us.

No bullying for us,

No, not in our school.

Remind the students of the time of their next session, when they will look more closely at what constitutes—and what are some more examples of—bullying behavior.

Session 3

Aim

To help the students define and enumerate bullying behaviors

Objectives

By the end of the session, the students will

- identify and create a list of bullying behaviors
- become more aware of bullying and its effects

Materials

- copy of the No-Bullying logo poster
- "Bullying Happens" poster from Session 2
- newsprint sheet (of bullying behaviors) from Session 1
- copy of the Bullying Behavior chart (Teaching Master 12) [For teacher use only.]
- newsprint and marker
- copies of "Mean Maddie" (Teaching Masters 5 & 6)
- sheets of poster paper
- colored markers or crayons
- copies of magazines and newspapers
- scissors

- paste or glue sticks

- tape

- stapler

Preparing for the Session

Carefully read through the entire session plan. Make copies of "Mean Maddie" (Teaching Masters 5 & 6) and carefully look over the poem. Following directions on page 24, make a sample booklet of "Mean Maddie" to show the students as they make their own during the session. Throughout the session, be cautious not to identify or imply by name any students who may be engaging in bullying behaviors or who may be victims of such behavior. Have sheets of poster paper, colored markers or crayons, copies of magazines and newspapers, scissors, paste or glue sticks, and tape on hand. Make a "Bullying Behaviors" poster by dividing a large sheet of newsprint into three columns as below:

Bullying Behaviors

Hurting someone's body or things	Hurting someone's feelings	Hurting someone's friendships

If as yet you haven't done so, take time to review the "What's Happening?" surveys the students completed in Session 2 and be ready to offer the students some feedback. Make a copy of the Bullying Behavior chart (see page 55). Review the chart prior to the session and have it handy for your own use as you lead the students through Step 4 in the session plan. See to it that the No-Bullying logo poster is displayed prominently in the meeting space.

Background for the Teacher

Studies have shown that bullying behaviors include not only forms of physical aggression, but also emotional harassment, social alienation, and both subtle and overt intimidation (the latter often being—but not exclusively—the behavior of girls who engage in bullying). No matter the type, bullying behaviors are usually difficult to detect. However, as a teacher, you need to be aware that all types of bullying occur at school. Likewise, it's also important to remember that bullying behaviors are *learned*. As such, they can be unlearned.

Session Plan

Beginning the Session

Gather the students in a circle. Draw attention to the copy of the No-Bullying logo poster. Then point out the "Bullying Happens" poster from Session 2 and ask one of the students to read it aloud.

BULLYING HAPPENS…

when someone with *greater* power

***unfairly* hurts someone**

with *less* power

over and over again.

Note: Keep this poster displayed in the meeting space for the remainder of the sessions.

Invite the group to recall the survey from Session 2. Take a moment to give the students some feedback about their responses to the survey. You do not have to be especially specific, but do offer some feedback to let the students know that you appreciate and value their input and honesty. Depending on the students' answers on the survey, you might say:

"According to the survey, bullying seems to happen a lot in the cafeteria. I have passed on this information to the principal."

or

"According to the survey, many of you don't really seem to know what to do when you see someone else being bullied. We will be doing some talking and learning about what to do."

Finally, to help the students recall some of the things they talked about that bullies do, ask:

• How can you tell if negative behavior (hurting another) is bullying? (*Look for responses that evidence understanding that bullying arises from a position of power and is repetitive.*)

Leading the Session

1. Display the "Bullying Behaviors" poster you made prior to the session.

Bullying Behaviors

Hurting someone's body or things

Hurting someone's feelings

Hurting someone's friendships

Invite the students to give some examples of behavior that might fit in each of the above three categories. List these behaviors in the appropriate columns on the poster. Assure the students that they will be discovering more of such behaviors in this session.

2. Distribute copies of "Mean Maddie" (Teaching Masters 5 & 6). Be sure to copy each master on a separate page. Direct the students to fold both Teaching Masters into fourths, and then to insert Teaching Master 6 into Teaching Master 5 to make an eight-page booklet. Check to make sure that the students have the pages in order so that the poem will follow and make sense. Provide a stapler to fasten the booklet pages together.

3. Depending on the size of your class, divide the students into small groups of two or three so that they all will have the chance to take part in reading the poem. Assign each small group to read one (or more) of the poem's fifteen stanzas. Give the small groups a moment to practice their reading aloud. Then have them come together to present a reading of the entire poem.

4. After the reading, invite the students to share their reactions to the poem. Then go on to draw attention once again to the "Bullying Behaviors" poster. Go through the poem, "Mean Maddie," stanza by stanza and have the students pick out and enumerate bullying behaviors, then list them under the appropriate column on the poster.

After reviewing the poem, encourage the students to suggest other bullying behaviors. As the students offer their suggestions, use your copy of the Bullying Behavior chart as a referent to suggest behaviors that could also be added to the poster.

Afterward, draw attention to the "Bullying Happens" poster to emphasize that the behaviors the students just listed are "bullying" *only when they are used **repeatedly** by someone with **greater power** over someone with **less power**.*

Tell the students that you will keep the "Bullying Behaviors" poster displayed in the room and that you will continue to use it (and add to it if necessary) to help them better recognize and deal with the problem of bullying in their school.

5. Have the students re-form the small groups they were in earlier. Give each small group a sheet of poster paper, colored markers or crayons, scissors, and paste or glue sticks. Make sure all the students have access to copies of magazines and newspapers. Direct the students in each small group to work together to design a poster that describes what bullying is. Tell them that they can use words, headlines or pictures from the magazines or newspapers, and/or their own art work to make the poster. Give the small groups time to work. Circulate to offer support, suggestions, or help where needed.

6. Invite each small group to present and explain its poster to the class. Be sure to congratulate the students on their cooperation. Help the students put up their posters in the meeting room. Explain that for the remainder of their sessions together, they can look not only to the "Bullying Behaviors" poster, but also to their own posters to help them remember what bullying is.

Concluding the Session

Gather the students in a circle around you. Set the copy of the No-Bullying logo poster on the floor in the center of the circle. Join the circle yourself and invite the students to join hands. Remind the students that you will send a "pledge" of support around the circle, a pledge that everyone in the circle can share, by *gently* squeezing the hand of the person on your right, who will then *gently* squeeze the hand of the person on his or her right, and so on, until the "pledge" of support goes all the way around the circle.

Once the "pledge" has returned to you, invite the students to show that they pledge to support no bullying in their school by taking a step forward—thus tightening the circle—and by reciting the No-Bullying pledge:

THE NO-BULLYING PLEDGE

Here in our school,

No bullying for us.

No hurting for us.

No unfairness for us.

No bullying for us,

No, not in our school.

Remind the students of the time of their next session, when they will discover why people engage in bullying behavior and how it affects their victims.

SESSION 4

Aim

To help the students develop empathy for the victims of bullying

Objectives

By the end of the session, the students will

- understand how being bullied feels

- increase their level of empathy for those victimized by bullying

Materials

- copy of the No-Bullying logo poster

- "Bullying Behaviors" poster from Session 3

- copies of "Feelings List" (Teaching Master 7)

- copies of "Acting Out Feelings" (Teaching Master 8)

- one copy of "Role Play Cards" (Teaching Master 9)

- newsprint and markers

- pens or pencils

- red pens or pencils

- optional: *Loudmouth George and the Sixth-Grade Bully* by Nancy Carlson; *How I Survived the Fifth Grade* by Megan Stine and H. William Stine (see pages 57 and 59)

Preparing for the Session

Carefully read through the session plan in advance. Make copies of "Feelings List" (Teaching Master 7), one for each student and "Acting Out Feelings" (Teaching Master 8), one for every two students. Make one copy of "Role Play Cards" (Teaching Master 9) and pre-cut the cards. Determine which students you could call on to present each of the role plays in Step 4.

> **Note:** Take care not to select likely victims or perpetrators of bullying to present the role plays. Likewise, during the session, be cautious not to identify or imply by name any students who engage in bullying behaviors or who are victims of such behavior. Have pens or pencils and red pens or pencils available. Consider using the Optional Activity. Be sure that the No-Bullying logo poster and the "Bullying Behaviors" poster are displayed prominently in the room.

Background for the Teacher

As an adult, imagine how you would feel if you were being harassed at work or were receiving threatening phone calls or were being stalked by someone. Surely, you'd feel annoyed, upset, angry, frightened, maybe even terrified. Your feelings would spur you to take evasive action to avoid the harassment, the threats, the stalking. So it is with children who are victims of bullying. These children devote enormous energy to avoid being bullied. Nearly all their activity at school is focused on getting and staying safe. Unfortunately, they cannot put an end to bullying on their own due to the intrinsic imbalance in bully/victim situations.

To end bullying and to help its victims, *all* the children need to understand and empathize with them. Too often, however, such empathy is channeled into aggression against the person who is exhibiting the bullying behavior. Unfortunately, this does little to end bullying. Children who bully are excited by victims who fight back and by aggression from others who "take the victim's side." As you lead the students through this session, take care not to allow the students' empathy for the victims of bullying to turn to aggression against those who are bullying. The goal is not to avenge victims of bullying, but to help them feel protected and safe at school.

Session Plan

Beginning the Session

Gather the students in a circle. Point out the small group posters on bullying that they made during their last session Step 5. Likewise, draw attention to the "Bullying Behaviors" poster and invite any student who wishes to suggest behaviors to add to it.

Leading the Session

1. Distribute copies of the "Feelings List" (Teaching Master 7). Ask one of the students to read the opening paragraph aloud. Go on to read aloud with the students all the feelings on the list. Afterward, pass out pens or pencils. Encourage the students—as a group—to come up with four more feeling words. Have the students add the words to the list.

   Finally, point out the directions on the bottom of Teaching Master 7. Give the students time to circle the feelings they remember. Then say:

   > " One of the most important things to know about feelings is this: Feelings come and go. No one is happy all the time. No one is sad all the time. No one feels excited all the time. No one feels bored all the time. Feelings are temporary and passing. This is important to remember when you're experiencing the ups and downs of growing up. Feelings will change. You can count on it."

2. Help the students find a partner. If someone is left out, pair up with him or her yourself. Give partners a copy of "Acting Out Feelings" (Teaching Master 8). Go through the directions with the students and then let them work together on the exercise. Afterward, call on partners to report on their experience. If you wish, ask questions like the following:

   • Was the acting out hard or easy to do?

   • Was guessing the correct feeling hard or easy?

   • What do you think is the best way to communicate how you're feeling to someone else?

3. Distribute red pens or pencils. Draw attention back to the "Feelings List." Tell the group that there are basically two types of feelings: *comfortable* feelings and *uncomfortable* feelings. Direct the students to look over the list

and to underline what they think are uncomfortable feelings. Then read the feelings aloud, one at a time. For each feeling, ask the students to raise their hands if they underlined it as being "uncomfortable."

Afterward, collect all pens and pencils.

4. To help the students recognize that people who are victims of bullying often end up having uncomfortable feelings most of the time, give the first of the "Role Play Cards" that you cut out from Teaching Master 9 to three students to present the role play. Allow two to three minutes for the presentation. Afterward, process the role play by asking questions like the following:

- What feelings do you think the person being bullied had?

- Do you think that person has a right to feel that way?

- Would you call those feelings comfortable or uncomfortable?

- How might you feel if something like this happened to you?

- Why would you feel that way? (Expect the students to recognize the unfairness of the bullying behavior.)

- How do you feel when you see someone else being bullied?

5. Go on to call on different students to present each of the three other role plays outlined on the "Role Play Cards." Use questions like those above to process each role play. Stress how the victim of bullying feels: threatened, alone, frightened, sad, powerless, etc.

To conclude, tell the students:

> "When we experience uncomfortable feelings, we want to do something about it. We want to change. Students who are victims of bullying can't always make changes on their own. They need help. They need my help and yours. They the help of *everyone* in our school."

Be sure to thank the students who took part in the role plays for their cooperation and good work.

Concluding the Session

Gather the students in a circle around you. Set the copy of the No-Bullying logo poster on the floor in the center of the circle. Join the circle yourself and invite the students to join hands. Remind the students that you will send a "pledge" of support around the circle, a pledge that everyone in the circle can share, by *gently* squeezing the hand of the person on your right, who will then *gently* squeeze the hand of the person on his or her right, and so on, until the "pledge" of support goes all the way around the circle.

Once the "pledge" has returned to you, invite the students to show that they pledge to support no bullying in their school by taking a step forward—thus tightening the circle—and by reciting the No-Bullying pledge:

THE NO-BULLYING PLEDGE

Here in our school,

No bullying for us.

No hurting for us.

No unfairness for us.

No bullying for us,

No, not in our school.

Remind the students of the time of their next session, when they will discover just the sort of help victims of bullying need to feel better and be safe at school.

Optional Activity

For a homework or "on your own" assignment, have the students read either *Loudmouth George and the Sixth-Grade Bully* by Nancy Carlson (suitable for fourth graders) or *How I Survived the Fifth Grade* by Megan Stine and H. William Stine (suitable for fifth graders). Have the students write a brief book report that answers the question, "How would you feel if you were George/Eliot?"

SESSION 5

Aim

To help the students recognize the distinction between tattling and telling in order to get help in a bullying situation

Objectives

By the end of the session, the students will

- define both tattling and telling

- understand the difference between tattling and telling

- recognize that they need to tell someone they trust about bullying to get help

- appreciate how adults in their school are willing to help stop bullying

- learn their school's procedure for reporting bullying behavior

Materials

- copy of the No-Bullying logo poster

- "Bullying Behaviors" poster from Session 3

- student copies of the "Feelings List" (Teaching Master 7) from Session 4

- one copy of "Role Play Cards" (Teaching Master 9)

- copies of "Burdens" (Teaching Master 10)

- copies of "Tattling vs. Telling: The Big Difference (Teaching Master 11)

- chalkboard and chalk or newsprint and marker

- pens or pencils

Preparing for the Session

Carefully read through the entire plan prior to presenting the session. Have the students' copies of the "Feelings List" (Teaching Master 7) from Session 4 on hand. Make each student a copy of "Burdens" (Teaching Master 10) and of "Tattling vs. Telling: The Big Difference" (Teaching Master 11). Make one copy of "Role Play Cards" (Teaching Master 9) and pre-cut the cards. Have pens or pencils available. Be ready to explain to the students the procedure your school has previously agreed upon for reporting bullying.

Carefully consider using the Optional Activity. Check to make sure that the No-Bullying logo poster and the "Bullying Happens" and the "Bullying Behaviors" posters are displayed prominently in the meeting space.

Background for the Teacher

Given the propensity of so many in society who "just don't want to get involved," it should come as no surprise that students are unwilling to get involved in dealing with bullying when they see it happening to another. Many students believe that telling adults about bullying will only make matters worse. In fact, that perception may well be the students' experience with bully/victim conflict, especially given the far too pervasive climate of tolerance and entitlement that has long surrounded bullying.

From early training, children—even the most caring—have been advised not to tell on others and to deal with conflicts on their own. This is good advice when the conflict is between individuals equal in power. However, it is not good counsel in a bully/victim situation, because the victim can never win. Thinking that a victim of bullying can resolve the problem on his or her own without help is like thinking a fourth or fifth grader can solve a problem in quantum physics without help.

In Session 4, the students discovered the plight of victims and learned to empathize with them. This session helps the students recognize that victims of bullying cannot handle bullying on their own. If they could, *they would have done so*. Victims of bullying need help, the help that comes from adult intervention. However, since adults in a school cannot always be aware of all bullying, and since bullying generally does not occur in the classroom, students must be encouraged to tell appropriate adults when it does occur.

Your challenge in presenting this session is to help the students recognize that it is appropriate to "tell" when they are being bullied or when they witness bullying, while discouraging tattling. An open and nonjudgmental attitude on your part will go a long way in helping students "tell," not "tattle."

Remember, students who are victims of bullying are afraid to tell. They fear both physical retribution and social ostracism. Make sure that the students understand that you and all school staff are committed to protecting the victims of bullying and that students reported for bullying will be watched and dealt with appropriately by you and others at your school and will be held responsible for any further bullying behavior.

Session Plan

Beginning the Session

Gather the students in a circle. Draw attention to the copy of the No-Bullying logo poster. Invite the students to recall the role plays from their last session. Then ask what they think would be the best thing to do if:

- they were being bullied

- they saw someone else being bullied.

Accept all reasonable replies. However, if the students suggest retaliation, point out that their channeling empathy into aggression against the person who is exhibiting bullying behavior does little to end bullying. Explain that students who bully are excited by victims who fight back and by aggression from others who "take the victim's side." Conclude by telling the students that in this session they will learn how to *tell* about bullying and get help without feeling that they're *tattling*.

Leading the Session

1. Divide the class into small groups of three or four. Give each student a pen or pencil and his or her copy of the "Feelings List" (Teaching Master 7) from Session 4. Give each small group a copy of "Burdens" (Teaching Master 10). Then display the "Bullying Behaviors" poster from Session 3.

   Invite the students to imagine that the tiny figure on "Burdens" (Teaching Master 10) is a victim of bullying. If you think it will be helpful, ask volunteers to describe a specific bullying situation, or use one of the bullying scenarios described on "Role Play Cards" (Teaching Master 9), for example:

   An older boy traps Noah in the hallway almost every day. He demands money, threatens to hurt him if he doesn't pay, and sometimes hits him.

Ask the students to tell what they notice about the picture on the worksheet. *(The victim is carrying a double load of burdens.)*

Give each small group the following directions:

(1) Choose from the list of bullying behaviors on the "Bullying Behaviors" poster and write the names of bullying behaviors in one of the bundles of the "victim's" load of burdens.

(2) Then, using your copies of the "Feelings List" (Teaching Master 7), find the names of feelings you underlined in red and write the names of these *uncomfortable* feelings in the bundles of the "victim's" other load of burdens.

When the small groups finish, have them share what they wrote. Collect the sheets to post later.

2. Use a small group's completed copy of "Burdens" (Teaching Master 10) to point out that someone who is being bullied carries a double load of burdens. First, the victim is weighted with the actual bullying behaviors themselves. Second, the victim also carries many uncomfortable feelings that are difficult to let go of or to change.

3. Help the students recall how, in their last session, they acted out feelings (see "Acting Out Feelings," Teaching Master 8). Ask:

• What did you find was the best way to communicate how you're feeling to someone else? *(to **TELL** someone)*

Write the word "Telling" on the board or newsprint and the word "Tattling" next to it. Acknowledge that people often use these words interchangeably, but stress that they do *not* mean the same thing. Invite the students to offer examples of telling and tattling. Record ideas on the board or newsprint.

4. Drawing on the ideas the students had about "tattling," help them recognize that tattling is speaking to someone about a problem:

• just to get somebody in trouble

• just to get their own way

• just to make themselves look good and somebody else look bad.

Explain to the students that when we do any of these things, we're tattling.

5. Go on to point out on the board or newsprint the ideas the students had concerning "telling." Help the students see that telling is speaking to someone about a problem in order to get help for themselves or for another.

6. Hand out copies of "Tattling vs. Telling: The Big Difference" (Teaching Master 11). Ask one of the students to read the first definition aloud:

> **Speaking to someone about a problem just to get someone else in trouble, to get my own way, or to make myself look good is _____.**

Then have the students write in whether they think the definition describes tattling or telling (answer: *tattling*).

Call on a different student to read the second definition aloud:

> **Speaking to someone I trust about a problem because I or someone else may be getting hurt is**
>
> **_____.**

Again, have the students write in whether they think the definition describes tattling or telling (answer: *telling*). Check both responses.

Take time to discuss the difference between tattling and telling. Encourage the students to offer examples of both tattling and telling. In the discussion, help the students understand that tattling gets someone *into* trouble, while telling helps get someone *out of* trouble.

As you conclude, draw the students' attention back to their copies of "Tattling vs. Telling: The Big Difference" (Teaching Master 11) and point out the incomplete sentence, "The big difference between tattling and telling is…" Direct the students to complete the sentence on their own. Afterward, check for understanding. Collect pens or pencils.

7. Display a completed copy of "Burdens" (Teaching Master 10). Explain that "telling" can help lift the "burdens" from the victims of bullying. Say:

> "If you are being bullied, or if you see someone else being bullied, the best thing to do is *tell* **a trusted adult in our school**."

Then go on to outline for the students the procedure your school has previously agreed upon for reporting bullying (e.g., *how* they are to report, *to whom* they are to report, *when and where* they are to report, etc.). Make sure the students understand that when they "tell" about bullying, their anonymity will be insured, re-emphasizing that an adult *will* step in to help and protect.

8. To practice using the school's procedures of "telling" to get help, divide the class into four small groups and give each group one of the "Role Play Cards" (Teaching Master 9) used earlier. Tell each group to use the situation described on its card to devise a role play that shows the right way to get help for the person who is the victim of bullying. Give the groups a few minutes to devise their role plays. Then allow two to three minutes for each presentation. After each presentation, take a moment to correct any misconceptions. Be sure to thank the students who took part in the role plays for their cooperation and good work.

Note: Consider arranging to have your class present all or some of these role plays to children in the lower grades in order to give them appropriate examples of "telling" to get help.

Concluding the Session

Gather the students in a circle around you. Set the copy of the No-Bullying logo poster on the floor in the center of the circle. Join the circle yourself and invite the students to join hands. Remind the students that you will send a "pledge" of support around the circle, a pledge that everyone in the circle can share, by *gently* squeezing the hand of the person on your right, who will then *gently* squeeze the hand of the person on his or her right, and so on, until the "pledge" of support goes all the way around the circle.

Once the "pledge" has returned to you, invite the students to show that they pledge to support no bullying in their school by taking a step forward—thus tightening the circle—and by reciting the No-Bullying pledge:

> # THE NO-BULLYING PLEDGE
>
> **Here in our school,**
> **No bullying for us.**
> **No hurting for us.**
> **No unfairness for us.**
> **No bullying for us,**
> **No, not in our school.**

Remind the students of their next meeting time. Tell them that when next they meet, the principal will join them to explain how the school will deal with those who bully.

Optional Activity

To enhance Step 7, create a "Bullying Report Card" to give each student as a reminder of your school's procedure for reporting bullying. Simply outline the procedure and have it duplicated on index cards or easy-to-carry sheets that the students can keep with them.

Session 6

Aim

To present school-wide consequences for engaging in bullying behaviors

Objectives

By the end of the session, the students will

- understand the meaning of consequences

- know the school-wide consequences for bullying

- better understand that all adults in the school are committed to making the school a safe and secure place

Materials

- copy of the No-Bullying logo poster

- "Bullying Happens" poster from Session 3

- "Bullying Behaviors" poster from Session 3

- chalkboard and chalk or newsprint and marker

- posterboard or newsprint and markers

- tape

- optional: index cards

Preparing for the Session

Carefully read through the session plan in advance. Prior to the session, use posterboard or newsprint to make a large poster entitled "Bullying

Consequences." With the aid and consensus of school staff, list your school's consequences for engaging in bullying behaviors. Arrange to have the principal in attendance to present the core of the session. Consider using the Optional Activity. See to it that the No-Bullying logo poster and the "Bullying Happens" and "Bullying Behaviors" posters are displayed prominently in the meeting space.

Background for the Teacher

Even the youngest of children can understand the concept of consequences. Unfortunately, many children have experienced how consequences are not fairly applied. They need powerful reassurance that your school has no tolerance whatsoever for bullying and that your school will impose swift and strict consequences when it does occur. *Trust* is what is at stake here. The students need to trust that responsible and caring adults will intervene in bullying behavior and keep them safe.

Session Plan

Beginning the Session

Invite the school principal to join with the students as they gather in a circle. Tell the students that the principal will be a visitor to their class today. Draw attention to the copy of the No-Bullying logo poster. Ask the students to explain its purpose. Afterward, go on to invite them to recall the difference between tattling and telling. Ask:

> What's the big difference between tattling and telling? (*Tattling gets someone into trouble; telling gets someone out of trouble.*)

Take time to correct any misunderstandings.

Ask one of the students to read aloud the definition of bullying on the "Bullying Happens" poster. Then, pointing out a few of the behaviors listed on the "Bullying Behaviors" poster, ask volunteers to explain how someone who is a victim of that behavior would feel. Finally, have the students explain how they could help themselves or someone else who is being bullied by *telling* a trusted adult.

Leading the Session

1. Have the students brainstorm the word "Consequences." Record ideas on the board or newsprint. Afterward, see if the students can come up with a

definition of "consequences" that reflects the understanding that consequences are what might happen after we say or do something.

2. To reinforce the students' understanding, have them suggest "what might happen" after each of the following scenarios:

   - You give your friend a birthday present that he or she really wanted.

   - You disobey your parents.

   - You have a yelling match with your sister or brother.

   - You shoplift.

   - You eat a whole box of chocolate bars.

   - You get straight A's on your report card.

   After the students respond, go on to tell them that their principal is going to talk to them about the consequences—about what will happen next—to people who bully others in their school.

3. The school principal will now address the students about your school's no-tolerance rule about bullying and about the consequences for engaging in bullying behavior. Make sure the principal has access to the "Bullying Consequences" poster you prepared prior to the session. The principal should also take time to reassure the students that school staff will support and protect victims of bullying.

4. When the principal completes his or her presentation, ask the students where they'd like to display the "Bullying Consequences" poster in their classroom. Then have the students post the list.

5. Briefly review the list of consequences. Let the students know that you—and all the other adults in the school—agree with the consequences, promise to be supportive to students who tell about bullying and want to end it in their school, and pledge to protect all victims of bullying.

Concluding the Session

Invite the principal to gather with the students in a circle around you. Set the copy of the No-Bullying logo poster on the floor in the center of the circle. Join the circle yourself and invite the students to join hands. Remind the students that you will send a "pledge" of support around the circle, a pledge that everyone in the circle can share, by *gently* squeezing the hand of the person on your right, who will then *gently* squeeze the hand of the person on his or her right, and so on, until the "pledge" of support goes all the way around the circle.

Once the "pledge" has returned to you, invite the students to show that they pledge to support no bullying in their school by taking a step forward—thus tightening the circle—and by reciting the No-Bullying pledge:

THE NO-BULLYING PLEDGE

Here in our school,

No Bullying for us.

No hurting for us.

No unfairness for us.

No bullying for us,

No, not in our school

If you wish, conclude with handshakes all around. Before dismissing the students, thank them for all their hard work and their willingness to end bullying in their school.

Optional Activity

To help the students remember the "Bullying Consequences," have them copy the consequences on an index card that they can keep and carry with them.

Teaching Masters

1. No-Bullying Logo Poster

2. No-Bullying Logos

3. Bully Not Wanted

4. What's Happening?

5. Mean Maddie

6. Mean Maddie (cont.)

7. Feelings List

8. Acting Out Feelings

9. Role Play Cards

10. Burdens

11. Tattling vs. Telling: The Big Difference

12. Bullying Behavior Chart

TM

```
┌ ─ ─ ─ ─ ─ ─ ─ ─ ─ ─ ┐
│                     │
│                     │
│                     │
│                     │
│                     │
│                     │
│                     │
│                     │
│                     │
└ ─ ─ ─ ─ ─ ─ ─ ─ ─ ─ ┘
```

Bully Not Wanted

Experience Necessary _____

_____

_____

Job Duties _____

_____

_____

Pay/Benefits _____

_____

_____

Do *Not* Apply At _____

WHAT'S HAPPENING?

1. I get bullied at school by being pushed, kicked, or hit.
   ☐ Never ☐ Once in awhile ☐ A lot ☐ Every day

2. I get bullied at school by name-calling, put downs, teasing, or being left out.
   ☐ Never ☐ Once in awhile ☐ A lot ☐ Every day

3. I bully others at school.
   ☐ Never ☐ Once in awhile ☐ A lot ☐ Every day

4. I think that most of the bullying that happens at our school happens
   ☐ in classrooms   ☐ in the bathrooms
   ☐ in hallways   ☐ in the cafeteria
   ☐ on the playground   ☐ on the school bus

5. I get bullied on my way to and from school.
   ☐ Never ☐ Once in awhile ☐ A lot ☐ Every day

6. When I'm in school, I worry about being bullied.
   ☐ Never ☐ Once in awhile ☐ A lot ☐ Every day

7. If someone bullies me, I usually
   ☐ Tell the bully to stop   ☐ Tell another student
   ☐ Don't do anything   ☐ Tell an adult at school
   ☐ Tell my parents   ☐ I don't get bullied

8. If I see someone else getting bullied, I usually
   ☐ Help the victim   ☐ Join in the bullying
   ☐ Tell an adult at school ☐ Tell another student
   ☐ Tell my parents   ☐ Don't do anything

9. To help me feel safe at our school, I think adults should
   ☐ Make rules about bullying
   ☐ Enforce rules about bullying
   ☐ Teach more lessons about how to get along better
   ☐ Have better supervision of:
      ☐ school bus   ☐ bathrooms
      ☐ school grounds   ☐ hallways
      ☐ cafeteria   ☐ classrooms

47

Cut off top at dotted line. Fold along lines to make a four-page booklet.

1

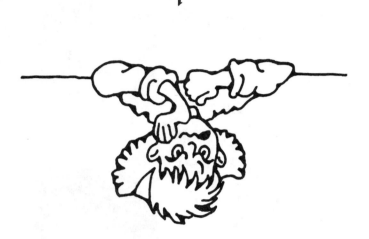

Mean Maddie

Nobody messed with Mean Maddie Stephen.
She always was on the attack.
Do something to her, and she would get even.
Mean Maddie got everyone back.

8

Well, let me tell you, nobody breathed.
They were sure that Mean Maddie'd go wild.
So, you can imagine the lunchroom's surprise
when Maddie blushed red and just smiled.

Ever since then, Maddie Stephen has changed.
Her bullying's come to an end.
We don't call her "Bully," or "Mean" anymore.
Instead, we just call her our friend.

Maddie liked fighting; she loved to do battle.
As an enemy, she was the worst.
If you wouldn't feud with Mean Maddie Stephen,
then she would just pick a fight first.

If someone was painting a picture at school,
Maddie'd look to see how he was doin' it.
Then, on purpose, she'd spill some inky black paint
all over the picture to ruin it.

2

"Guess what?" the kid said, "I won't be afraid
of all of the bullying you do.
Besides," the kid smiled, "I talked to the teacher,
and she says her eye is on you.

"So I think that maybe we could be friends.
Then you won't have to yell, scream and slug.
I forgive you for punching me out," the kid said,
then reached over and gave her a hug!

7

5

Over and over, Mean Maddie was mean.
So some of us called her a bully.
I bet if you'd known her that you'd be afraid,
and that you'd agree with us fully.

So all of us kids kept our distance from Maddie.
To cross her would be a big error.
Maddie was tough, and Maddie was mean.
Maddie was one holy terror.

4

Then one day, this new kid came into our class
and made the most awful boo-boo.
While riding his skateboard a little too fast,
he bumped and knocked down "you know who."

"Forgive me," he said, "I'm sorry I hurt you."
Maddie just sat there and steamed.
"I'm sorry," he said, "here, let me help you."
"Don't touch me, you creep!" Maddie screamed.

Mean Maddie stood up screeching and yelling,
called the kid names, then she got him.
She hauled off and hit him with all of her might
and knocked the kid flat on his bottom.

Well, everyone figured that he'd learned his lesson.
He'd felt Maddie's mean knockout punch.
Imagine the shock, when the next day at school,
he sat down next to Maddie at lunch!

6

Maddie spread rumors and gossiped about
others to get them in trouble.
She never built up; she always put down,
and turned many a friendship to rubble.

If kids got upset or told her to stop,
Maddie'd call them a bunch of cry babies.
Then she'd get the kids back; she'd make fun,
    or tease them,
or hit them—no ifs, ands, or maybes!

3

Feelings List

Do you know what? "Good" or "bad," "right" or "wrong" are not names of feelings. Nope. They're judgment calls about feelings. Feelings aren't "good" or "bad," "right" or "wrong." Feelings just are. It's okay to feel the way you feel. However, it's not always easy to name what you're feeling. But you can do something about that. You can expand your feelings inventory. Here's a list of feeling words to help you recognize and identify the feelings you're having.

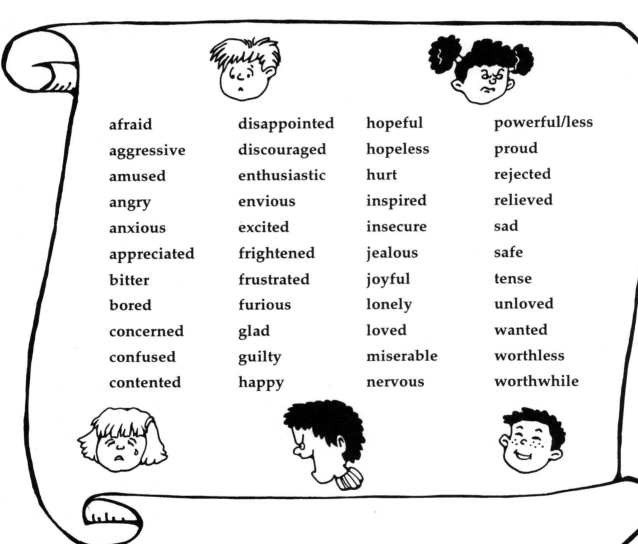

afraid	disappointed	hopeful	powerful/less
aggressive	discouraged	hopeless	proud
amused	enthusiastic	hurt	rejected
angry	envious	inspired	relieved
anxious	excited	insecure	sad
appreciated	frightened	jealous	safe
bitter	frustrated	joyful	tense
bored	furious	lonely	unloved
concerned	glad	loved	wanted
confused	guilty	miserable	worthless
contented	happy	nervous	worthwhile

Wow! Quite the list! And there are many other feeling words, too. See if you can add four more feeling words here.

_____   _____   _____   _____

Acting Out Feelings

Sit face-to-face with a partner. Take turns acting out one of the feelings you circled on the "Feelings List" by using body language only. The partner who is watching must try to "read" or understand the body clues and figure out what feeling his or her partner is trying to act out.

When you act out a feeling, begin by using the least amount of body language possible. Only gradually add clues or make the clues bigger and more understandable.

Reverse roles and repeat the exercise with another feeling.

After each partner has had at least two turns in acting out feelings, use the following questions to discuss the exercise:

- Was it difficult to tell the difference between some of the feelings? (Note: Many feelings "look" the same.)

- What's the best way to communicate how you're feeling to someone else? (Clue: Unscramble these letters L E T L.)

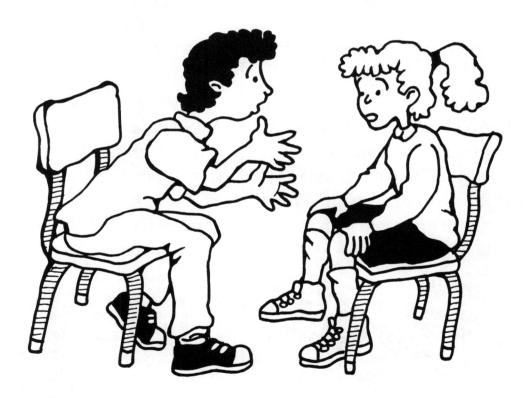

1

Brian has to wear special, thick glasses. The glasses make Brian squint. Two other boys in Brian's class are picking on him and calling him names.

2

Cheryl is trying to eat her lunch. A bigger and older girl is grabbing food off her tray and threatening to beat up Cheryl if she tells.

3

An older boy traps Noah in the hallway almost every day. He demands money, threatens to hurt him if he doesn't pay, and sometimes hits him.

4

A new girl has joined the class halfway through the year. She wants to make friends. She wears clean, but older clothes. Three of the "in" girls in class tease her about her outfits. They shut her out, whisper about her, and laugh at her.

Speaking to someone about a problem just to get someone else in trouble, to get my own way, or to make myself look good is

_____.

Speaking to someone I trust about a problem because I or someone else may be getting hurt is

_____.

The big difference between tattling and telling is...

_____

_____

_____

_____

_____

Bullying Behavior Chart

	Physical Harm to another's body or property		**Emotional** Harm to another's self-esteem		**Social** Harm to another's group acceptance	
LEVELS	**verbal**	**non-verbal**	**verbal**	**non-verbal**	**verbal**	**non-verbal**
1	Taunting Expressing physical superiority	Making threatening gestures Defacing property Pushing/shoving Taking small items from others	Insulting remarks Calling names Teasing about possessions, clothes	Giving dirty looks Holding nose or other insulting gestures Saying someone has germs or is unclean	Gossiping Starting/spreading rumors Teasing publicly about clothes, looks, etc…	Passively not including in group Playing mean tricks
2	Threatening physical harm Blaming victim	Damaging property Stealing Initiating fights Scratching Tripping or causing a fall Assaulting	Insulting family Harassing with phone calls Insulting intelligence, athletic ability, etc…	Defacing school work Falsifying school work Defacing personal property, clothing, etc…	Insulting race, gender Increasing gossip/rumors Undermining other relationships	Making someone look foolish Excluding from the group
3	Making repeated and/or graphic threats Practicing extortion Making threats to secure silence: "If you tell, I will…"	Destroying property Setting fires Biting Physical cruelty Making repeated, violent threats Assaulting with a weapon	Frightening with phone calls Challenging in public	Ostracizing Destroying personal property or clothing	Threatening total group exclusion	Arranging public humiliation Total group rejection/ostracizing

Bullying involves exploitation of a less powerful person. There must be an unfair advantage being exerted. Bully/victim conflict is best understood as a dynamic relationship. Whether or not a behavior is bullying depends on its effect upon the victim. This chart was designed to assist with the identification of bullying behavior in situations where an unfair advantage exists. The seriousness for all levels of behavior should be evaluated based on the harm to the victim and the frequency of the occurrences.

Additional Resources

The following materials are available from the Johnson Institute. Call us at 800-231-5165 for ordering information, current prices, or a complete listing of Johnson Institute resources.

No-Bullying Program Materials

Tee shirts with the No-Bullying logo displayed on the front, posters, stickers, and extra teaching manuals for your school may be ordered simply by calling the sales department at Johnson Institute.

Video Programs

An Attitude Adjustment for Ramie. 15 minutes. Order #V429

Anger: Handle It Before It Handles You. 15 minutes. Order #V450

Broken Toy. 30 minutes. Order #V462

Choices & Consequences. 33 minutes. Order #V400

Conflict: Think About It, Talk About It, Try to Work It Out. 15 minutes. Order #V451

Dealing with Anger: A Violence Prevention Program for African-American Youth. 52 minutes (males), 68 minutes (females). Order #V433 (for males); Order #V456 (for females)

Double Bind. 15 minutes. Order #V430

Good Intentions, Bad Results. 30 minutes. Order #V440

It's Not Okay to Bully. 15 minutes. Order #5883JH

Peer Mediation: Conflict Resolution in Schools. 28 minutes. Order #V458Kit

Respect & Protect: A Solution to Stopping Violence in Schools and Communities. 28 minutes. Order #V460

Tulip Doesn't Feel Safe. 12 minutes. Order #V438

Publications

Bosch, Carl W. *Bully on the Bus.* Order #P413

Boyd, Lizi. *Bailey the Big Bully.* Order #P422

Carlson, Nancy. *Loudmouth George and the Sixth Grade Bully.* Order #P414

Crary, Elizabeth. *I Can't Wait.* Order #P431

———. *I'm Furious.* Order #P506

———. *I'm Mad.* Order #P509

———. *I Want It.* Order #P427

———. *My Name Is Not Dummy.* Order #P429

Cummings, Carol. *I'm Always in Trouble.* Order #P418

———. *Sticks and Stones.* Order #P420

———. *Tattlin' Madeline.* Order #P421

———. *Win, Win Day.* Order #P419

Davis, Diane. *Working with Children from Violent Homes: Ideas and Techniques.* Order #P244

DeMarco, John. *Peer Helping Skills Program for Training Peer Helpers and Peer Tutors.* Order #P320Kit

Estes, Eleanor. *The Hundred Dresses.* Order #P411

Fleming, Martin. *Conducting Support Groups for Students Affected by Chemical Dependence: A Guide for Educators and Other Professionals.* Order #P020

Freeman, Shelley MacKay. *From Peer Pressure to Peer Support: Alcohol and other Drug Prevention Through Group Process.* Order #P147-7-8 (for grades 7, 8); Order #P147-9-10 (for grades 9, 10); Order #P147-11-12 (for grades 11, 12)

Garbarino, James, et al. *Children in Danger.* Order #P330

Goldstein, Arnold P., et al. *Aggression Replacement Training: A Comprehensive Intervention for Aggressive Youth.* Order #P329

Haven, Kendall. *Getting Along.* Order #P412

Johnsen, Karen. *The Trouble with Secrets.* Order #P425

Johnson Institute's No-Bullying Program for Grades K–Middle School. Order #546Kit

Julik, Edie. *Sailing Through the Storm to the Ocean of Peace.* Order #P437

Lawson, Ann. *Kids & Gangs: What Parents and Educators Need to Know.* Order #P322

Mills, Lauren A. *The Rag Coat.* Order #P417

Moe, Jerry, and Peter Ways, M.D. *Conducting Support Groups for Elementary Children K–6.* Order #P123

Olofsdotter, Marie. *Frej the Fearless.* Order #P438

Perry, Kate, and Charlotte Firmin. *Being Bullied.* Order #P416

Peterson, Julie, and Rebecca Janke. *Peacemaker® Program.* Order #P447

Potter-Effron, Ron. *How to Control Your Anger (Before It Controls You): A Guide for Teenagers.* Order #P277

Remboldt, Carole. *Solving Violence Problems in Your School: Why a Systematic Approach Is Necessary.* Order #P336

———. *Violence in Schools: The Enabling Factor.* Order #P337

Remboldt, Carole, and Richard Zimman. *Respect & Protect®: A Practical Step-By-Step Violence Prevention and Intervention Program for Schools and Communities.* Order #P404

Sanders, Mark. *Preventing Gang Violence in Your School.* Order #P403

Saunders, Carol Silverman. *Safe at School: Awareness and Action for Parents of Kids in Grades K–12.* Order #P340

Schaefer, Dick. *Choices & Consequences: What to Do When a Teenager Uses Alcohol/Drugs.* Order #P096

Schmidt, Teresa. *Anger Management and Violence Prevention: A Group Activities Manual for Middle and High School Students.* Order #P278

————. *Changing Families: A Group Activities Manual for Middle and High School Students.* Order #P317

————. *Daniel the Dinosaur Learns to Stand Tall Against Bullies. A Group Activities Manual to Teach K–6 Children How to Handle Other Children's Aggressive Behavior.* Order #P559.

————. *Trevor and Tiffany, the Tyrannosaurus Twins, Learn to Stop Bullying. A Group Activities Manual to Teach K–6 Children How to Replace Aggressive Behavior with Assertive Behavior.* Order #P558

Schmidt, Teresa, and Thelma Spencer. *Della the Dinosaur Talks About Violence and Anger Management.* Order #P161

Schott, Sue. *Everyone Can Be Your Friend.* Order #P435

Stine, Megan, and H. William Stine. *How I Survived 5th Grade.* Mahwah, NJ:Troll Associates, 1992. Order #P415

Vernon, Ann. *Thinking, Feeling, Behaving.* (for grades 1–6) Order #P250

Villaume, Philip G., and R. Michael Foley. *Teachers at Risk: Crisis in the Classroom.* Order #P401

Wilmes, David. *Parenting for Prevention: How to Raise a Child to Say No to Alcohol/Drugs.* Order #P071

————. *Parenting for Prevention: A Parent Education Curriculum—Raising a Child to Say No to Alcohol and Other Drugs.* Order #PO72T

ORDER FORM

<table>
<tr><td>

BILL TO:

Name _____

Address _____

_____

City _____ State _____ Zip _____

ATTENTION: _____

Daytime Phone: (____) _____

PURCHASE ORDER NO. _____

❑ Individual Order ❑ Group or Organization Order

If Ordering for a Group or Organization:

Group Name _____

</td><td>

SHIP TO: (if different from BILL TO)

Name _____

Address _____

_____

City _____ State _____ Zip _____

ATTENTION: _____

Daytime Phone: (____) _____

TAX EXEMPT NO. _____

Please send me a free copy(ies) of Johnson Institute's:	❑ ___ Publications and Films Catalog(s) ❑ ___ Training Calendar(s) ❑ *Observer*, a quarterly newsletter

</td></tr>
</table>

PLEASE SEND ME:

QTY.	ORDER NO.	TITLE	PRICE EACH	TOTAL COST

For film/video titles, please specify: ❑ 1/2" VHS   ❑ 3/4" U-Matic   ❑ 1/2" Beta   ❑ 16mm

SHIPPING AND HANDLING		
Order Amount	**U.S.**	**Outside U.S.**
$0–25.00	$ 6.50	$8.00
$25.01–60.00	$ 8.50	$10.00
$60.01–130.00	$10.50	$13.50
$130.01–200.00	$13.25	$19.50
$200.01–300.00	$16.00	$24.00
$300.01–over	8%	14%

Please add $8.00 ($10.50 Canada) for any videotapes ordered.

OFFICE USE ONLY

Order No. _____

Customer No. _____

QVS, Inc.

❑ Payment enclosed
❑ Bill me
❑ Bill my credit card:

❑ MasterCard
❑ VISA
❑ American Express
❑ Discover

[ ][ ][ ][ ][ ][ ][ ][ ][ ][ ][ ][ ][ ][ ][ ][ ]

Expiration Date: _____

Signature on card: _____

Total Order _____
(Orders under $75.00 must be prepaid)

6.5% Sales Tax _____
(Minnesota Residents Only)

Shipping and Handling _____
(See Chart)

TOTAL _____

Have you ordered from the Johnson Institute before? **Yes** ❑   **No** ❑
If yes, how?   **Mail** ❑   **Phone** ❑

JOHNSON INSTITUTE®

7205 Ohms Lane ❖ Minneapolis, Minnesota 55439-2159
(612) 831-1630 or toll-free: 1-800-231-5165